My Life in Tangents

Lucyann Davis

Presentation by *BookLeaf Publishing*

Web: www.bookleafpub.com

E-mail: info@bookleafpub.com

ISBN: 9789360945350

First edition 2024

This dedication goes out to my favorite teachers: To Mrs. Wood for teaching me to love poetry, To Mrs. Silverman for teaching me to love reading. And to Mr. Beebe for giving me the music that became the soundtrack of my life. I would not be here if not for you.

ACKNOWLEDGEMENT

I'd like to thank everyone for believing in me and my ability to get the writing challenge done!

PREFACE

This little collection of poems started out as an experiment in commitment. I was to write a poem for each of the 21 days to accomplish the experiment. Sometimes I wrote every night. Sometimes I wrote 2 poems in one night so I could have the next evening free. I did it and I'm thrilled!

The Mighty Niagara

The water swiftly rushes by,
Thundering as it leaps over the edge,
Cascading towards the rocks
Crashing upon impact
Spitting out fallen branches
Mesmerizing onlookers
As it races towards its destination.

Wounded Souls

We are two wounded souls through no fault of
our own,
The pain flows out of us in misdirected anger,
It's never meant towards each other,
However, the inability to process pain is the
cause,
Others don't understand and see the anger in a
different light,
But we are meant to help each other and vowed
to do so.
Our lives are entwined for good and bad,
Life is complicated and sometimes sad.

Nugget

3

Bouncy and cheerful,
So fluffy and cuddly,
Maltipoo Nugget!

Upside Blue

Blue is the breeze whispering through the
summer sky,
Blue is a warm hug from a newborn pup,
Blue is the mountains meeting the horizon,
Blue is the ocean so deep and wide,
Blue is the eyes that envelope me in love.

Asymmetrical

Not identical,
Misshapen and all askew,
Asymmetrical.

Deafening Silence

Silence can be so loud when a heart is aching,
Unheard screams deafen from the inside,
Trapped in my head as if paralyzed.
Why can't I speak?
Why can't I move?

At Peace

Slipping downstream with the sun on my
shoulders,
Paddling close to the edge of civilization,
I wander where the stream takes me,
And smile at the blue sky above,
I breathe in the smell of giant spruce trees,
I glide past the pines and feel the breeze,
As it caresses me,
And envelopes me in peace.

Nature's Tap Dance

Dark and dreary, gray everywhere I turn,
The rain plays a concerto on the skylight,
Clouds collide with a loud boom,
Interrupting my daydreams by the fire,
I glance up as light darts across the sky,
A rainbow in the distance makes me smile.

Weekend Getaway

Maybe a cottage by the ocean,
Or a cabin in the woods,
It doesn't really matter,
As long as we're together,
You take my highs,
I'll take your lows,
We can work it out,
Even if it's just for a weekend.

Seafaring

The wind whispers in my ear,
Calling me to shore,
Where the sails are puffed up,
Pulling at the mooring,
Jumping onboard I untether her,
And we're off—
Gliding across the sea.

Daybreak

Shrouded in darkness,
The trees rustle,
Sharing secrets with one another,
One by one the birds call out
To invite others to sing along,
In the distance, an owl bids adieu,
Ready to hunker down for his day's rest,
The sun tiptoes into the sky,
The moon slips into a slumber,
Daybreak has arrived.

Life is Like Dodgeball

A sneak attack hurtling in your direction,
But you dodge swiftly out of the way,
Sometimes catching the ball,
Then launching it away,
Keeping your eyes on the ball,
You glide to your right,
Your opponent is foiled!
And just then from out of sight,
Comes a ball knocking the wind out of you.
Now you must pick yourself up and start again.

Come Clean

It's time to come clean,
And bare my soul,
To share my heart's desire,
It's time to be brave,
And speak out,
To do what's best for me,
There's no time for fear,
The clock is ticking.

Just Jump!

One foot in and one foot out,
Curious today,
I jump into what can be!

First Snow

Dainty crystals float down from above,
Gently dusting trees nearby,
Becoming a lattice blanket on the hills,
While covering window sills,
Untouched and beautiful,
Soon to be a shovelful.

Fading

Fading like the sunset,
Quietly into the darkness,
Once a thrilling rush of energy,
Once but no more,
Dreams dashed upon the floor,
Slipping into oblivion.

A Tree

For many,
A tree is just a tree,
But not to me,

A home for feathered friends,
Shade on a sunny day,
Brilliant on the holiday,

Giving us a guarantee,
Of all the air we need,
Caring for the trees,
Should be decreed.

The Ladder

Under a blanket of darkness,
No moon in the distance,
Appears a crystal ladder,
Beckoning the wistful,
To take that climb,
To the clouds above,
Ushering them to heaven's doorstep,
Gently the door opens,
To be greeted by a loved one,
To get a bear hug,
And a kiss goodbye,
Upon waking,
The warmth of the hug still lingers.

The Flowered Box

There's a pretty flowered box,
Hiding in Grandma's attic,
It's tied up in pink ribbons,
With a tag labeled dreams,
No one has touched it in years,
Forgotten; collecting dust,
I ache to untie the ribbons,
And reach inside,
To steal a glance,
At Grandma's belongings,
But I mustn't!
It wouldn't be right,
To intrude on her precious dreams,
I take a deep breath,
Turn and walk away.

Misfit

Always on the outside looking in,
Never included; never fit in,
The harder I try,
The worse the fit,
Only when I don't care,
Do I get somewhere,
Time to put the blinders on,
Time to breathe deeply and carry on.

Don't Ask

Don't ask for special treatment,
If you can't do the same,
Don't expect extra attention,
When you barely glance my way,
How can you care,
If you don't share.

www.ingramcontent.com/pod-product-compliance
Lightning Source LLC
La Vergne TN
LVHW050250200726